Haz

Find me hiding
throughout the book

"My Mum says it's okay if I don't share ALL the time...but it doesn't stop other people always wanting what is mine."

"Give it to me now Haz,
you've got to share
you know..."

"...it's not just yours to play with, other people want a go."

"My Mum says I don't have to share if I'm halfway through a game..."

"Haz, can I have that teddy now,
you've had it all day long.
I promise I won't lose it,
not sharing it is wrong..."

"My Mum says I don't have to share this toy...

...it's my special one you see..."

"I've had it all my life and don't want anyone touching it, but me."

"Haz, let me do that puzzle too,
I really want a go..."

"...I'll show you where
to put the pieces,
you're going way too slow."

"I'd like to do this puzzle alone, when I'm done I'll give it to you..."

"...my Mum says I don't have to share if I'm in the middle of learning something new."

"When it comes to asking me to share,
my sister Ava is the worst..."

"...she always seems to want the toy that
I was playing with first."

"Mum says giving her what she wants straight away won't help her to learn, that if someone's already playing with something, she might have to wait her turn."

"Haz, can you get off and push me now,
that looks really fun..."

"I'm happy to take turns Ava,
but my go has just begun..."

"Mum says I don't have to share what
I'm playing with straight away.
Try your best to be patient or find
something else to play."

"My Mum teaches me every day how to be polite and caring..."

"...and that being kind to others doesn't have to involve sharing!"

"She has taught me how to show respect and that I deserve it too..."

"Playing with others can be fun...
but I don't HAVE to share with you!"

Printed in Great Britain
by Amazon